Ab

MW01095113

Twenty-five years ago, "networking" was an undefined, frivolous activity. As a marketing representative for the Wilshire Chamber of Commerce in Los Angeles, California, Mel Kaufmann quickly became aware that most members were leaving chamber events without any new business. For the next two years, he would arrive at the chamber office at 5 a.m. and think of processes he could teach to enhance members' revenue. During these two years, he discovered 100 "Little Miracles," and each had the potential to increase profits. Kaufmann began to teach new members "Little Miracles" and the seminars became so successful that he has taught them throughout the U.S. and the world. Over time, he transformed "networking" from grade school to the grad school of relationship building.

Dedication

This book is dedicated to God
because there was no other
source available.

Thinking of you...

*Perpetual
Prosperity
Mel*

Perpetual Prosperity

Perpetual prosperity is a practical technology. Zoroaster taught it to the fire worshipers over three thousand years ago. All the spiritual masters through the centuries taught it. The prophets down through the ages have taught, "Do unto others, as you would have others do unto you." Any teaching that has lasted for over 150 generations must have great power. There is nothing new about *Perpetual Prosperity*. The only thing new is that professionals are beginning to use it. My mission is to have people gather their business friends together and share the wisdom in **Little Miracles**, as Zoroaster gathered his people over 30 centuries ago, to share the wisdom of the ages. If this *Pious Platitude* has been relevant in people's spiritual lives for centuries, it must also be viable in people's business lives today. When people care as much about their friends' careers as they do about their own, they will receive prosperity beyond their wildest dreams. **Little Miracles** has transformed a *Pious Platitude* to a *Practical Principle*.

Little Miracles
A Journey to Financial Freedom

One hundred
little business
miracles
as
never before
revealed

Definitions

A **Little Miracle**:
- A financial truth that never varies.

Networking:
- The exchange of ideas, information, and resources.

A Link defined:
- A professional who bonds with another professional to exchange productive information consistently and immediately.

A Link imperative:
- A Link must have a similar Rolodex but market a different product or service.

Clusters:
- The cobbling of **Little Miracles** to determine who is a Link possibility (**Little Miracles 66-73**).

Two definitions of an event:
1. An organized group of business people
2. When two or more people meet

The Networking Process

Networking is an easy four step process that anyone can learn. Let this quick start process begin your Journey to Financial Freedom. Read, apply and share all 100 miracles to reach Financial Freedom.

1. Planning
  Miracle-21 - Prepare a Game Plan
  Miracle-24 - The Calendar of Cash
  Miracle-64 - Prepare for Events

2. Attend
  Miracle-1 - Be Early
  Miracle-4 - Time-Wasters
  Miracle-6 - The Resourceful Registrar

3. Actively Network & Make Connections
  Miracle-3 - How do you Pick and Choose?
  Miracle-66 - The Bridge
  Miracle-65 - The Clusters
  Miracle-79 - The Five Minute Waltz
  Miracle-93 - Talk to Everyone

4. Manage Contacts *(Use EspressoBrain.com Online Tools)*
  Miracle-28 - Tithe to Your Links
  Miracle-88 - Begin Each Appointment With a Gift
  Miracle-59 - Love Your Links
  Miracle-60 - Be A Dream-Maker

Repeat The Process

Signup and use the EspressoBrain Café ™ to manage contacts, relationships and PAKs.

Little Miracles
The Table of Topics

Little Miracles
The Table of Topics

Little Miracles
The Table of Topics

Little Miracles
The Table of Topics

Miracle 1

Be Early

I am not talking about protocol. I am talking about making more money. I am talking about bottom-line profits. Most of us have been admonished from a toddler, "Don't be late." You have had many mentors. Several mentors come to mind. They are your mother, your father, your teachers, and your employer. No one has ever explained the financial advantages of being early. The **Little Miracles** will address the value of being early. Vince Lombardi, the late coach of the Green Bay Packers, shared a benevolent truth: "If you are ten minutes early, you are late." My commandment is, unless you are thirty minutes early to events, you're late. I have asked many people, "Why be early?" The answers I get are legion "I get the best parking spot." Or, "I get the best seat." Or, "I get the biggest bagel." These reasons do not add one more comma to your paycheck. Being late is a Monetary Mistake.

Be early, stay late

Miracle 2

Pick People

An important reason for being early is to pick and choose the *Productive People* you need to meet. This is the same principle used in choosing the best parking spot, the best seat, or the biggest bagel. Only this time you are choosing professionals who can provide the biggest and best business opportunities for you. When you begin to use the **Little Miracles**, you begin to realize that preparation and planning are in order. You now enter an event with an agenda. You must become aware you are not talented enough to wing it. Only birds can do that. You have to supply scaffolding on which to hang all of your studied and honed networking skills. If there are one hundred people attending an event, you cannot meet them all in a 30-minute Social Hour, so you have to pick and choose. The next question is, "How do you pick and choose?" Read on, dear friend.

Pick your people, pick your destiny

Miracle 3

How do you pick and choose?

The question for **Little Miracles** seekers is, "How do you pick and choose the person you need to meet?" The answer is to arrive at each event thirty minutes early, pay your dues, make out your name tag, register for the event, greet the registrar, greet the host, and greet the speaker. After you enter, stand fifteen feet from the entrance and face the door at a 45° angle, so you don't look like a hungry financial vulture. Keep your eyes riveted on each person's name tag. Do not judge people's dress. Do not judge their hair style, their jewelry, or their bodily contours. Continually focus on their name tag. Look for the firm name, the person's name, and the position of the stranger. Look at the picture, not the frame, because, if you become enamored by the frame, you will miss the financial picture.

Priceless picture, worthless frame

Miracle 4

Time-Wasters

Be aware of the time you waste. I will share four time-wasters. The first time-waster is standing in the registration line. The long line seems interminable. Standing in the registration line is a total waste because the person in front of you is from your office and that person is not only a time-waster but a hindrance. Your friend keeps you from meeting others. You don't meet the person behind you because you are involved with your friend. The second time-waster is checking in with the registrar. The third time-waster is waiting to pay your dues. The fourth time-waster is making out your name tag. The twenty minutes you take to register is a financial waste because you have not used your networking time wisely. You now enter the event twenty minutes late. These are squandered minutes of precious networking time.

Squander time, squander money

Miracle 5

Lost Loot

The ten minutes you lost in the registration line, the four minutes checking in with the registrar, the three minutes paying dues, and the three minutes making out your name tag add up to twenty minutes of lost revenue. This is money that will never *Tickle your Till*. If a thief reached into your pocket and stole a $1000 bill, you would be furious and you would probably call Colombo. But if you come late to an event and waste precious networking time, the result is the same as if a thief picked your pocket. This stolen loot is gone, never to return. Only this time you have stolen from yourself. Like the arrow shot from a bow, the *Lost Loot* will never return to your networking quiver. When you steal from yourself, you never complain because you are not aware the loot was stolen. Unaware people sully my psyche.

Lost Loot is Lost Luxury

Miracle 6

The Resourceful Registrar

The registrar must be more productive than just giving you your name tag, signing you in, and collecting your dues. Being thirty minutes early gives you the opportunity to get acquainted with the registrar. The registrar is an important cog in your financial sprocket. Treat the registrar as you would your best client because the registrar knows everyone you need to know. The registrar can introduce you to the sponsors of the event. The registrar can introduce you to the hosts and hostesses of the event. The registrar can introduce you to members you should know. The registrar is the person closest to the executive director of the association. The registrar can introduce you to the executive director. The registrar can introduce you to the speaker. The registrar is one of the most important people at each event you attend. The registrar becomes your unpaid salesperson.

A registrar rings your register

Miracle 7

Greet the Executive Director

G reeting the executive director IS transparently clear. If you embody this **Little Miracle**, you will no longer just have lint at the bottom of your pockets. You will have *Wads of Wealth* in your wallet. Think on this, the executive directors often advise the affluent in selecting a financial consultant, an accountant, a lawyer, an architect, a construction professional, an insurance agent, a physician, a dentist, and dozens of other service providers. The executive director is your Link to a myriad of wealthy executives and business owners. The key in your *Quest for Cash* is to have the executive director use you as a resource person for the association and their affluent members.

Go from Oblivious to Obvious

Miracle 8

Influence the Influential

You do not influence the influential by selling your services to the influential. With your unlimited talents, think of ways you can be of service to the executive director in his or her duties to the members of the association. If you are an accountant, volunteer your services to keep the association's books. If a lawyer, volunteer to be the association's legal counsel. Be a resource person, screen suppliers, help with the advertising, help with their public relations, help supply speakers for their monthly meetings, and volunteer to address one of the association meetings. The key to unlimited wealth is to earn the trust and confidence of the executive director. The director is now a conduit to each member of the association or organization. When you influence the influential, your income will rise like dough in a baker's oven.

Become indispensable

Miracle 9

The Learned Lecturer

Don't be intimidated by the learned lecturer When you approaching the speaker, don't assume it's an imposition. Socrates said, "Question assumptions never before doubted." One of the financial advantages of being early is to meet and learn from the speaker before the presentation begins. You came to the event to gain knowledge. The speaker has knowledge. Therefore, go up to the speaker with alacrity. Remember: do not sell your wares. Do not talk about your product or service. Never enter an event without an agenda. Spend your precious minutes with the speaker by asking some questions. Have your speaker questions prepared and memorized. Ask the speaker some information-gathering questions. You will leave the event with more information than anyone who attended the event.

Intimidation needs permission

Miracle 10

Powerful Professionals

After the presentation, walk up and stand by the *Powerful Professionals* standing by the speaker. The well-connected professionals gather around a prominent speaker. Many of these *Powerful Professionals* are Link possibilities. There will be a comma in the conversation. Be patient, extend your hand, introduce yourself, and ask some probing business questions about each professional's business. Again, be prepared and rehearsed. Gather a few business cards and your revenue journey has begun. Once begun, your revenue journey never ends.

Powerful Professionals Produce

Miracle 11

Tardy Tales

Being late for events is an unconscious act. It is called unconscious incompetence. Most people are clueless. Everyone has their tardy tales. Everyone has an excuse for being late. Some people want to enlarge their ego. An enlarged ego shrivels the pocketbook. Excuses are legion. Some people mention traffic. Some mention a last-minute phone call. Others mention they are disorganized. Others mention poor planning. Some are reluctant to participate. These are reasons not truths. The next **Little Miracle** will peel the onion down to its financial core. Read the next **Little Miracle** with enthusiasm, insight, understanding, and respect.

Develop Conscious Competence

Miracle

Low Priority

There is only one reason for being late to any event you are attending. The one reason for being late is low priority for the event. That is the primary reason for being tardy and I can prove it. If I were to offer you $100,000 to enter the next event sixty minutes early, would you be late? Not on your life! You would have stayed at the event all night so you would not miss the deadline. I have good news! This is not like the gaming tables in Las Vegas because there is no risk. Every event you attend is filled with a multitude of business opportunities for you. Use the **Little Miracles** and you will accumulate over a million dollars of net worth over your life time. I would not give you one penny for your *Tardy Tales.*

Eliminate tardy from your tales

Miracle 13

Classic Clumps

If you enter an event and see nothing but *Classic Clumps* of professionals, you blew it! You were late. You have to take responsibility for your penury. This is another business reason for being early. Professionals do not enter in clumps. The entrance is too narrow. Professionals enter as animals boarding Noah's Ark. Business people enter at least two at a time. This is the time you greet the important people you came to meet. Be prepared! Have a few business questions ready. Executives who do not return your phone calls will talk to you as they enter an event. This is another little business **Little Miracle**.

Clumps are circles of fear

Miracle 14

What is Networking?

Everyone believes they network but no one can define it. What you can't define you can't control. You can't enter your financial orbit with your Links unless you use the same economic launching pad. I found the definition of networking I use in a book by John Naisbitt. The title of the book is *Megatrends*. John discusses ten mega-trends – ten mighty trends that will transform business as we enter the 21st Century - and chapter eight is all about networking. Naisbitt peeled away the contours of networking with his definition. He defined networking as, "The exchange of ideas, information, and resources." It is that simple. This very instant, put down this book and call or e-mail one **Little Miracle** to a friend. Now you are networking!

A shared idea is worth millions!

Miracle 15

Networking and Selling Don't Mix

Networking and selling are like oil and water. They are both vital for your financial engine, but keep them in separate containers. Some professionals equate networking with selling. This is a false assumption. I have often heard people say as they leave a luncheon, "Boy, am I a good networker! I got three new prospects." That is not networking. That's selling. Networking bonds a relationship. Selling inhibits a relationship. Selling creates a wall. Selling separates people. Unless you have taken the vow of poverty, stop selling at events. If you keep asking for the order, at the next event you attend, people you want to meet will avoid you as if you had a *Virulent Virus*. Begin gathering information, not deals.

Networking makes selling obsolete

Miracle 16

Stop Networking

Stop networking at events. Begin pre-networking. Pre-networking is gathering information. Networking is the exchange of ideas, information, and resources. You do not have the luxury of time at an event to share information. I continually pre-network. Stop networking and begin gathering information. You have a thirty-minute window of opportunity when you attend an event. The social time from 11:30 until noon is your information-gathering opportunity. When you gather information, you uncover Links. When you uncover Links, you uncover money. Remember, linking creates multiple business opportunities. Selling inhibits a multitude of business opportunities.

Stop gathering deals, gather Links

Miracle 17

The Compliment of Cash

Why continually add compliments to each communication exchange? Because it works! It not only makes the other person feel better but it also makes your bank balance feel better. I will share an experience with you about how I made over $80,000 by giving one compliment. In 1991 I gave a seminar in Los Angeles for a national CPA firm. The day after the seminar I called their marketing director. I thanked her for sponsoring the event. I also mentioned that without her I would not have had the opportunity. Before she hung up she said, "Send me another packet about your seminars. I will send it to our national marketing director in New York City." Within six months I was sitting across the desk from the national marketing director in New York City. I have been conducting seminars for PriceWaterhouseCoopers ever since. That was over fifteen years ago.

Cash in on a compliment

Miracle 18

The Questions of Yesterday

Most professionals ask yesterday's questions. These questions go nowhere. Make a 180° paradigm shift in your conversations. Let me quote some yesterday's questions I continually hear "Did you watch the game last night?" "How's your golf game?" "How are the kids?" "How's the wife?" These questions form a financial cul de sac. You go around and around and end where you began. Nowhere! If you add up all the business you have missed in your life, you could be on the beach in the Bahamas this afternoon. The following are three keys to unlocking profitable information: 1) Begin each conversation with a question. 2) Use prepared questions. 3) Apply intelligent listening. These three keys form a trilogy of opulence. If you do not change your yesterday questions, you will become stunted like a tree that has held onto its leaves too long.

Stop living in yesterday

Miracle 19

Conversation Control

Begin every conversation with a question. When you begin any communication exchange with a question, you are in control of the conversation. You can control the information you need. If you want to know about the ball game last evening, ask a gaming question. If you want to know if that person is a possible Link, ask **The Clusters Questions** (refer to definition page). Never enter an event without a prepared game plan. If you wait until you shake the hand of a stranger to develop a communication plan, the network game is over before it begins. Remember; every network event begins with a question and ends with information. This **Little Miracle** may be hazardous to your indigence.

Ask, don't tell

Miracle 20

Know Who is Coming to Dinner

I t is no longer "GUESS who is coming to dinner." It's "Know who is coming to the event." Let's begin with why most professionals attend events and gain no financial edge. Most professionals attend events for five wrong reasons: 1) They are a member. 2) They like the speaker. 3) They were asked by a friend. 4) They were given a ticket. 5) They feel obligated. Eliminate these financial errors. If you are planning to attend for business development reasons, read on. If not, give your **Little Miracles** to a truth seeker. If these **Little Miracles** make financial sense, keep reading.

When hunting ducks, go to a pond

Miracle 21

Prepare a Game Plan

A reason for not gaining a financial edge is because professionals don't prepare a game plan. I want to share a true story of the value of this **Little Miracle**. Over a quarter of a century ago, I wanted to present a networking seminar to Deloitte & Touche. For two years no one from Deloitte would return my phone calls. I was determined to crack the CPA industry. I prepared a game plan. I read in the Los Angeles Business Journal that Deloitte & Touche was sponsoring a seminar at the Beverly Hilton Hotel. I attended the seminar. I met the speaker because I was early (**Little Miracle 1**). He liked my concept of marketing. I conducted a seminar for Deloitte and the rest is history.

The future belongs to the prepared

Miracle 22

Research Your Audience

Research your audience. Another wrong reason for not gaining a financial edge is because most professionals do no research. Before I attended the seminar given by Deloitte, I did my research. I discovered accountants loathe the word selling. They prefer *Practice Development*. It does something to their endorphins. I arrived sixty minutes early. There was only one person in the auditorium; the speaker. A partner of the firm. He and I were the only people in the auditorium. He didn't have a chance because after a few minutes he asked what I did. I answered, "*Practice Development*" and he was hooked. We had lunch and within ninety days I was asked to conduct a seminar for their firm at the Beverly Hilton Hotel in Beverly Hills, California. This is not the end of the saga. Read on and observe the cascading effect. As you read on another **Little Miracle** will be revealed.

Custer did not research his audience

Miracle 23

The Ripple Response

The partner at Deloitte & Touche was so impressed with my seminar he contacted the AICPA in New York City and suggested I be a speaker at the next CPA convention in New Orleans. I was chosen. I received the highest rating of all the break-out speakers. I spoke to over three hundred CPAs and marketing directors. And more than twenty five years later I am still conducting seminars for CPA firms all across the United States and Canada. I have made $110,000 over the years from CPA firms all because I was early once, a quarter of a century ago! That is more than a ripple effect, it is a waterfall. These **Little Miracles** will inspire you both professionally and personally.

The Ripple Response is Relentless

Miracle 24

The Calendar of Cash

Peruse your periodicals. Search for local business opportunities. Search for The Calendar of Events. This is a list of all the business events taking place in your community each week. The Calendar of Events includes the name of the speaker, the speaker's topic, the sponsor, the contact person, and their phone number. I have a marketing commandment. Attend one event every week for the rest of your career and use **The Cluster Questions** (refer to the definition page) at each event and you will be on your path to independent wealth. Arthur Martinez, the former chairman of Sears, wrote, "There is no national law that says we have to have a recession."

Use the Calendar for Cash

Miracle 25

Who Will Attend?

Before attending any event, determine who will be attending whom you need to know. I want to share three options: **1)** Call the office of the event sponsor and have them e-mail the reservation list to you. **2)** If they are too busy, check their web site. **3)** If they are too busy, go to the sponsoring office and look over the list. This is not a privileged list, if you are considering attending. You will discover three key items on the reservation list: the professional's name, the firm name, and the phone number. You will discover at least two professionals from a firm you need to know. Trust this **Little Miracle**.

Why wait for Karma?

Miracle 26

Know Who to Know

Check the registration list. First, look over the list with a microscope and look for professionals with Link potential. Second, look for a group of professionals who are prospects. Check Links first and prospects second. Always think Links first. Of all the professionals on the list, determine which will make the best Links. Your competition will not go out of their way to get a reservation list. Your competitors will not think Link. Your competitors will not think prospect. Your competition will think friend. Your competition will think failure. A Link leverages your time and money exponentially.

Today determines your tomorrow

Miracle

Research

After deciding which executives you wish to meet, I give you ten research assignments: **1)** Google 'em. **2)** Study their industry periodicals. **3)** Learn the industry jargon. **4)** Drop by the executive's office. **5)** Pick up a brochure. **6)** Pick up some collateral material. **7)** Learn the name and position of the executive attending. **8)** Learn the names and positions of other executives in upper management. **9)** Obtain periodicals from their association office. **10)** Ask others in your business community what they know about the firm, the executives, and upper management. You will be head and torso above your *Complacent Competition.* Unless your competitors have studied the **Little Miracles**, this method of research has never crossed their *Business Brain.*

Every audience is predictable

Miracle 28

Tithe to Your Links

In the ancient scrolls, the high priests asked for all to give 10% of their crops to the Temple. This was not a suggestion it was an edict. This giving was called a tithe. Farmers were doing so well when they tithed, after a decade it became voluntary. Tithe to your Links. Don't give money or crops to your Links give 10% of your time. Six minutes out of each hour of each day fax, phone, or e-mail some productive information to your Links. If you have twelve Links, and they do the same for you, you are receiving twelve times more information than you are giving. All of us soon learn information has a way of turning into clients and clients into crisp new folding money. If your boss asks you to get back to work when you are tithing to your Links, just say, "Sorry, boss. I can't right now. I am too busy tithing."

Your tithing dice are always loaded

Miracle 29

Information is Power

Information is power. Information is economic power. A paradigm shift is in order. Shift your paradigm 180°. Realize that information is more important than a client, a customer, or a prospect. Valuable information is multiple clients, customers, or prospects. A client is singular. Productive information is multiple business happenings. Your assignment is to search for information that will become a myriad of clients, customers, or prospects for you and for your Links. You will discover productive information in your local business journal, your local business periodicals, your business friends, and the local *Pub Proprietor*. Peter Drucker said,

"Money is information in action".

Miracle 30

Information is Not Power

This **Little Miracle** does not conflict with **Little Miracle 29**. After a Link seminar in New Orleans, a participant came up to the podium and said to me, "Information is not power. Applied information is power." He was telling me that applied information becomes *Prosperity Power*. That made economic sense to me. An educator once stated, "For a person who won't read and a person who can't read, the result is the same. Neither learns." So a person who has information and does not apply it is no different from a person who does not have information. Your assignment is not only to gather information but also apply it and share it. No information left behind.

Ignorance is resistance to learning

Miracle 31

Beyond Applied

Applied information is a cottage in the country. Shared information is a mansion on the hill. Shared information is the beginning of a relationship. A relationship is the end of separation. Shared information completes the information circle of gathering and sharing. Information has ultimate revenue enhancement power, when it is applied and shared. Information that is not shared produces financial cholesterol. It clogs your financial arteries. Develop twelve Links. When you share a business-bit with twelve professionals, you will receive twelve bits of information in return. If my mathematics is correct, that is a 1200% return on your investment of time. Your ROI will beat the Dow every time.

Information has consequences

Miracle 32

The Financial Iceberg

Ninety percent of all the information you need for success is beneath the surface. I call this information beneath the obvious. A multitude of business fortunes lie undetected beneath the frozen obvious. I was conducting a seminar in Chicago for the American Marketing Association (AMA). After the presentation a woman asked, "Are you aware that there are 1500 associations with their headquarters in the city of Chicago and they are all looking for speakers?" I got financial goose bumps. There were fifteen hundred associations looking for speakers. That is 1500 times more revenue opportunities than if she had commented, "Call me. I know someone who wants to attend your next seminar." Information is the 90% of your financial iceberg. This is a prime example of information being more *Professionally Potent* than a referral and it is beneath the obvious.

Your future is beneath the obvious

Miracle 33

Never Sit by an Associate

If you sit by an associate or a friend, you are a loser. Strangers do not approach you because they feel they would be intruding on your *Financial Frivolity*. Never sit by someone from your office. They don't buy from you and they don't sell to you. You don't need their business card. Answer this question: "Why do you do it?" Your answer most likely is, "It's comfortable." My question to you is, "Do you want comfort or cash?" It is your decision. Sitting by a friend is not wrong. Sitting by a friend is not right. It just doesn't make any economic sense. This networking error is like a razor-sharp sword, it has two edges. Number one; you do not reach out to others. Number two; others do not approach you. Both of these sharp edges cut into your annual revenue. Now you have become a double-edged *Link Loser*.

Eliminate your Poverty Parables

Miracle 34

The Baggage of Yesterday

Don't make a habit of sitting by a friend. Sitting by a friend is yesterday's baggage. Ernest Holmes wrote, "Never limit your view of life by past experiences." Do you want to be in bondage to a friend or a host to a stranger? A friend keeps you in shackles. A friend keeps you in financial prison. A friend keeps your tether too short. Then you will miss your financial goodies. Break the bond. Be incarcerated no more. Five years from now 50% of all your business will come from people you have yet to meet. A stranger opens the door to unlimited possibilities. Be financially free of the baggage of yesterday. Change the habit now because if you wait, two days from now, tomorrow will be yesterday.

Yesterday ended last night

Miracle 35

Don't Ignore That Stranger

Have you ever sat by a stranger who was talking to their friend and you were totally ignored? How did this experience make you feel? One man in Portland, Oregon, said, "Being ignored makes me feel about one inch tall." When you ignore a stranger you are lowering their self-esteem. No one has the God-given right to lower another's self-esteem. If we have any right at all, it is to raise others' self-esteem. And guess what? When you raise others esteem, your self-esteem goes up along with theirs. Like water, self-esteem seeks its own level. A thought: any time you feel your self-esteem is low, take time to raise the self-esteem of the next person you meet. Your self-esteem will thank you.

Ignore no more forever

Miracle

Sit Between Two Strangers

Sitting between two strangers is like Wrigley's gum: it doubles your business pleasure. It is not like Las Vegas because there is no gamble. You cannot lose. I don't want anyone to play a game where anyone loses. When you use the **Little Miracles** you leave everyone a winner! To multiply your opportunities, look at the firm name on each stranger's name tag before you sit down. Make sure each person you sit by is a financial opportunity for you. Sit between two strangers once a week for four weeks and you will discover at least two Links. This **Little Miracle** has promise.

Little Miracles will amaze you

Miracle 37

Meet Both Strangers

Don't get so enamored by stranger number one that you forget to introduce yourself to stranger number two With this error is a double edge loser. First; you will lower the self-esteem of the professional you ignored. Second; the person you ignored may have a Rolodex full of your future clients. You do not know the financial value of either stranger until you have used **The Clusters Questions** (refer to the definition page) with both of them. Gather productive information from both strangers: then you can determine if one or both are business possibilities. Get their cards and give at least one a call tomorrow. Miss no opportunity!

Eliminate Stranger Danger

38 Miracle

Stranger to Stranger

This may be more important to your future than **Little Miracle 37**, because helping others achieve their goals and dreams is vital to your career. You have to give beyond core service. Everyone gives core service. Zoroaster taught his fire worshipers over 3000 years ago, "Do unto others as you would have them do unto you." Those who do not give will have a difficult time finding givers. Most marketers I know have forgotten the first part of the Golden Rule and only remember, "Do unto me." If you are always asking for the order, you have taken a scissors to the rule that is golden and removed the first and most important part, "Do unto others." Ray Kroc was quoted as saying, "The way to get rich is to help everyone around you get rich." Zig Ziglar so simply said, "The way to get what you want is to help others get what they want." Need I add another syllable?

Do unto others has legs

Miracle 39

Winning on Empty

An empty chair has no redeeming value. An empty chair does not answer questions. An empty chair does not ask questions. An empty chair does not have business cards. An empty chair does not purchase products. An interior designer in New Orleans told me this story: "I came into an event and looked for a seat. I looked for the firm name on the name tags. I noticed a developer. I filled the empty chair beside him. We began a relationship. Within 90 days I had signed a $175,000 contract to design the interior of his next commercial project." Don't allow any space between you and your dreams.

An empty chair is full of dreams

Miracle
Sit by Design

Always have a game plan for every event you attend. Few people enter an event with a game plan. Stop doing as other do. Have a well-constructed design. Cut a new swath. Abraham Lincoln so brilliant stated, "A towering genius disdains a beaten path." Know before you leave your office who will be your luncheon partner. **Little Miracle 20** explains the method to use to determine your *Breakfast Buddy*. It is such a financial wasteland to sit by a person who can be of no financial value to you or your career. If you had eliminated all the time you wasted at business events sitting by unproductive people, you would be *Relaxing on the Riviera*. Read **Little Miracle 41** to discover how to select a seating partner.

Seat control is money control

Miracle 41

Never Sit at an Empty Table

When you sit at an empty table, you have lost control of your luncheon partner because someone will soon come over to your table and ask you, "Is this seat taken?" You have no choice but to say, "No, won't you join us?" This is like playing *Russian Roulette* because if you find a relationship by sitting at an empty table, it is an accident. Turn the tables on the tables. Determine during the Social Hour which professional you wish to sit by. Let that person sit first, then go to that person and ask "Is this seat taken?" That person will automatically say, "No, won't you join us?" Now you are in control of your own financial destiny. Now you have at least ninety revenue enhancing minutes. And controlled minutes have a mysterious way of turning into money.

Have more Money Moments

Miracle 42

Attend One Event a Week

Walk through your fears. Fear is simply a learned response. It's a habit. If you have a bit of trepidation when meeting strangers, this **Little Miracle** will allay your fear of those unknown beings. Attend one event a week where you don't know anyone and don't take anyone. The people you meet are called "strangers." The principle reason for being fearful of meeting strangers is because most people are unprepared and unrehearsed. Rehearse **The Clusters Questions** (refer to the definition page). The best remedy for fear is to *Prepare and Practice*. Practice and practice and practice some more. Shakespeare wrote over four hundred years ago, "Act the part and become it." Ralph Waldo Emerson stated in 1849, "Do the thing you fear and the death of fear is certain."

Fear nothing, understand everything

Miracle 43

The Sixty-Second Intro

Within sixty seconds after entering a meeting shake hands with a stranger. When you meet strangers, you are preparing for the future. The majority of your peers seek out a friend. They exchange a few pleasantries, gather some *Gooey Gossip*, and parrot yesterday's news. When the gavel comes down to begin the meeting, the only thing your peers have accomplished is to convert *Meetings to Musings*. The have failed to convert *Meetings to Money*. Your peers are clueless. I have a suggestion. Introduce yourself to a stranger within sixty seconds after you arrive at an event. Use **The Cluster Questions** (refer to the definition page). Then follow by introducing the stranger to a friend. You have helped each person broaden their financial base and everyone wins! Repeat the process until the gavel hits the sounding board and continue this **Little Miracle** until you retire or expire.

Plan more stranger moments

Miracle 44

The Letterman Lunch

In the 1920s, Elmer Letterman was an insurance salesman in New York City. He reserved a table for four at the Four Seasons Hotel five days a week. He would call a friend, client, or prospect and ask who they would like to meet. He would arrange a luncheon for no more than three guests. His plan was to help his friends, clients, and prospects develop contacts that would enhance their careers. He carried no brochure. He carried no rate book. He sold no insurance. If anyone asked him about insurance, his comment was always the same: "My partner will give you a call." Because of this process, Elmer became a millionaire. With this **Little Miracle** you are frustrating tradition. Break down the prison walls of tradition.

Light another's candle

Miracle 45

Beyond Your Profession

Find an organization beyond your profession and you will find prosperity. An empirical study shows that 31% of professionals belong to an organization beyond their profession. And only 50% of the 31% are in a productive organization or association. I call this *collective insanity*. That means that 84% of professionals either join no organization or are in an organization that is not producing financial results. If you are not a member of any civic organization, now is the time to select and join an organization or association. Los Angeles has over 1800 civic associations or organizations to choose from. This includes American Heart, American Lung, American Cancer, American Diabetes, United Way, Girl Scouts, Boy Scouts, a multitude of Chambers of Commerce, and on and on. These associations have offices in every city in America.

Follow the money, not the crowd

Miracle 46

The Careful Organization

Most of your peers join an organization because there is an opening, or a friend says an association needs you. These are not reasons for success. They are reasons for failure. Just because everyone is doing it does not make it prudent. Let me share four solutions: **1)** Obtain a membership roster from several associations. Check to see if the members are professionals you want to rub shoulders with for the rest of your career. **2)** Select six associations to visit. **3)** Visit all six of your selections to discover which association has the most professionals who can enhance your career. **4)** Join. The dues you pay are cost-effective marketing. You are also giving back to the community where you are making your fortune.

Have more planned happenings

Miracle 47

The Careful Event

When I was in marketing at a chamber of commerce in Los Angeles, the chamber had at least 17 events annually. These events were breakfasts, luncheons, dinners, golf tournaments, tennis tournaments, etc. I have four suggestions for attending productive events: **1)** Make your decision by who is attending rather than which event you most enjoy. **2)** Look at the reservation list. **3)** Determine who will attend. If those attending a golf tournament are the professionals you need to spend more time with, polish your putter and go! **4)** After the tournament, visit the 19th hole. The 19th hole may be where you hit the green.

Use the chamber for commerce

Miracle

Choose One Committee

Never join a civic organization without becoming involved. Involvement is where bonding begins and bonds are nurtured. If you are flipping pancakes next to the CEO of IBM at a homeless shelter, you will bond. It is inevitable. This means you must have an agenda. Know which committee members will be holding a pancake spatula. From the members attending, determine by whom you want to flip pancakes. When you are flipping and sweating, you are bonding. You are beginning a relationship. Remember, you are the CEO of your own financial universe. There is an immutable principle: when you give to the less fortunate, the Universe is always generous.

Choose a committee for cash

Miracle 49

The Careful Committee

Each committee has different members and different functions. Check <u>two</u> committees to join. The first committee is the membership committee. This is a powerful *Money-Making* committee. You not only learn of the new members before your competition, but you also meet dozens upon dozens of prospective members. Even if these prospective members don't join your association, you have met them! Because you met them, you will have the opportunity to use **The Cluster Questions** (refer to the definition page) and you may discover a potential Link. The second committee is the fund-raiser committee. Think on this for a moment. Whom will you meet if you become a fund-raiser for an association? Wealthy patrons! If you want more affluence, become a fund-raiser. As a fund-raiser, executives who would not return your phone calls will talk to you. Again, be sure you use **The Clusters Questions**.

When you serve, you are served

Miracle 50

The Unlimited Potential

There is unlimited potential within your staff. I gave a marketing seminar to a small CPA firm in San Diego. They brought in all their staff. This included the secretaries, the receptionist, the administrator, the janitor, and the computer programmer. They invited everyone on their payroll. I taught each of the staff the **Little Miracles**. Then they all were sent to different functions in San Diego. Within a few months the receptionist was bringing in more business than the managing partner. I concluded that you do not have to have an accounting degree, a law degree, or be a graduate of an MBA program to develop new business. With the **Little Miracles** training, you will brand your community. However, this takes continual training, continual practice, and continual monitoring of your entire staff.

Branding is not just for cows

Miracle 51

Organizations are Different

If you want to cover your financial community like a blanket, each of your staff must attend a different organization or association event. When using **The Cluster Questions** (refer to the definition page) your staff will return to your office with enough information to *Bomb your Business.* If each of your staff follows **The Cluster Questions** week after week, month after month, and year after year, your competition will only see your contrail. No one can make a move in your community without your firm discovering this productive information first. When you are number one with productive information, you are number one with prosperity.

Sew a community quilt

Miracle 52

The Puppy Prescription

The advice I am about to give cannot be learned in any MBA program in America. If you could only regain the love of a puppy you have buried deep within since childhood, you could not handle all the business. I have a *Puppy Prescription* for you. Enter a room wagging your tail with enthusiasm, excitement, and glee. Know no stranger. Give affection and attention to all. Have apt attention. Are nonjudgmental. Withhold no love. Love everyone unconditionally. Hold no grudges. Have total self-esteem. Do not accept being ignored. Always be happy. Never complain. Sue no one. Take no depositions. Be not concerned by the Dow Jones. Do not worry about a recession. Always be truthful and totally honest. Hold no resentments. Greet everyone as a friend. Then all work becomes *Puppy Play*.

This prescription has unlimited refills

Miracle 53

The Entire Organization

The marketing department is not the entire organization but the entire organization must be the marketing department. I would print business cards for all your staff. Print cards for everyone from the janitor to the CEO. Eliminate no one. You never know who your janitor may know. The old adage is still relevant: "Everyone is only three people from the person you need to know." Realize everyone on your staff knows someone who needs your product or service. I remember when I was in real estate in Seattle in the early '70s, I worked with the late President Nixon's younger brother.

Everybody is somebody's something

Miracle 54

It's Who Listens

It's not who talks. It's who listens. When you decide to attend an event, determine the audience as well as the speaker. The speaker may be dull but the audience may be brilliant. The event may be filled with professionals you need to know. This takes some creative thinking. For example; if the Secretary of Labor was giving a lecture in your city tomorrow, should you take the time and money to attend? The audience would be labor leaders, firms that employ labor, professors from the surrounding universities, CEOs, owners of businesses, wealthy individuals, and the entire real estate industry. My question is, "Should you attend?" If any of these professionals are important cogs in your wheel of fortune, cancel everything and go!

An audience is predictable

Miracle 55

Shyness No More

There are no strangers, only friends we have not met. Think of a good friend. Are you shy and hesitant when you meet that friend now? At one time that friend was a stranger. Think of the next stranger you meet as a friend you have not met. Shyness no more forever! Shyness is self-imposed. It is important to know my definition of shy: "A person who is reluctant to approach a stranger." Make a mental decision to replace shyness with openness. Shyness is a habit. Shyness is not inherited. Shyness is not in your DNA. A physician does not tell a mother in the delivery room, "We have a problem here. Your kid is shy." If they are not shy when born, then it is a learned response. A learned response can be unlearned. William James wrote, "We must become dis-inhibited." Neale Donald Walsch taught, "Life begins at the end of your comfort zone." Reach beyond your boundary lines. Stretch your limits of opportunities.

The high cost of low esteem

Miracle

Greet Strangers as Friends

Greet strangers as friends. Behavior modification is in order. This may be a stretch. It is time we all add more stretch marks. Develop a new habit of greeting strangers with the same enthusiasm as you greet friends. With enthusiasm you will attract money as the honeysuckle attracts a bee. Think of your life as a movie. Project yourself on a screen with the same enthusiasm you now convey when meeting a stranger. Ask yourself this question, "Would you buy from you?" If the answer is "No," add enthusiasm. The word enthusiasm is a fascinating word. Actually it is a combination of two words, from the Greek words En-theo. En means within. Theo means God. When you are expressing enthusiasm, you are expressing the God from within.

God within, you're not without

Miracle 57

Assuming is a Process

Assuming is a process. Socrates over 400 years BC wrote, "Question assumptions never before doubted." Question everything and everyone. When you continue to ask questions, you will live in the state of constant amazement. I quote from *The Celestine Prophecy* "Do not leave anyone until you know why you were brought together." Assume everyone you meet has valuable information for you. Therefore, use **The Cluster Questions** (refer to definition page) everyone. Question the janitor, the bag person at the supermarket, and the CEO of a Fortune 500 company. The secret of financial power is to be a constant inquisitor. When you gather productive information from everyone, a metamorphosis takes place. Like a caterpillar becoming a butterfly, information becomes green, rectangular strips of parchment.

Only assume a 2% mortgage

Miracle 58

Giving Creates a Void

Giving creates a void the Universe rushes in to fill. I learned this in high school physics. The experiment was to take a gallon can and suck all the air out of the container. It collapsed. I learned the reason. The Universe keeps pressing until the pressures are equal and then it rests. I concluded from this physics experiment that the Universe cannot tolerate inequities. When you give you will receive. You cannot change this immutable law of the Universe. The reverse is also true, when you receive the Universe requires you to give. When you don't give, you don't receive. The Universe is simple. In fact, you have no options. That's just the way God put the Universe together. You can't improve upon God's equation.

Create more voids in your life

Miracle

Love Your Links

A Mighty Mystic over 2000 years ago admonished his followers, "Love your neighbor as yourself." I ask you to love your Links as yourself. Think of your Link's success as an extension of your own. Let me give you my definition of love: "To assist another in fulfilling their dreams." This applies to your children, to your wife, to your husband, to all your personal relationships, and to your professional relationships. This is almost an impossible assignment. If you care for your Links' future as you care for your future, you will receive a continuous *Business Bounty*, pressed down, shaken together, and overflowing. This moves you from grade school to the grad school of networking.

Include love in your job description

Miracle 60

Be a Dream-Maker

It is impossible to help others reach their dreams and their goals unless you know their dreams and their goals. The best way to learn your Links' dreams is to ask. Ask your Links, "What are some of the professional dreams you want to achieve in the next five years?" Don't accept "I want to travel." or "I want to retire." or "I want to surf off of the Barrier Reef." Discover if they want to expand their firm into other cities. Discover if they want to expand their products or services. Discover if there are any business people they would like to meet. Discover if they want to sell their business. Discover what they want to do after they retire. Then it is your task to do all you can to help them fulfill their goals and dreams. Form a strategic alliance with all your Links.

Be a dream-maker, not a dream-taker

Miracle 61

The Duke of Ellington

My daughter Racquel told me recently, "If you want to lead the orchestra turn your back on the crowd." Duke Ellington was often spotted sitting on his suitcase in the back of a Pullman car writing his music. His musicians were sipping Scotch and playing poker. He became a legend. His musicians became intoxicated. The choice is yours. You can spend time with your associates sipping fermented barley or become a solitary giant in your industry. Stop doing what does not get you where you want to go. Socrates, over 2400 years ago so insightfully penned, "Break the crust of convention." Use your time in the quest of becoming a legend.

Becoming a legend is a choice

Miracle 62

Selective Giving

You cannot give to all the business people in your community. You do not have the time, expertise, or the energy. Professional giving is unlike personal giving you have to be selective in your professional giving process. How do you determine which professionals to give to? Your decision is determined by the business questions you ask. Ask **The Cluster Questions** (refer to definition page). The answer to The **Cluster Questions** determine which professionals have Link potential. After only four Link questions you will know who has the Link possibilities. Cement a relationship before you begin the selective giving process.

Giving unites

Miracle 68

Communication is a Choice

Miracle 68 is the beginning of your Link questions. You must not only memorize these *Laser Link* questions before you leave your office, you must commit them to memory, embody them, and move them from your *Mind to your Molecules*. When you shake hands with a stranger, you must know the direction of the communication exchange. Communication is a choice. You either choose to ask business questions or talk trivia. It is up to you. If you don't talk business, you have lost the networking game before it begins. You have only one time at bat. Don't strike out! When you apply the four Link questions, you will hit at least one economic home run at each event.

Communication is not chance

Miracle 64

Prepare for Events

There are six requirements TO complete five days before an event: **1)** Know the information you need to gather. **2)** Know who will be attending. **3)** From those attending, determine which professionals you want to know. **4)** Research the professionals and the firms you want to know. **5)** Rehearse **The Cluster Questions** (refer to definition page). **6)** Prepare a one-sentence answer to a question you may be asked about your firm. Then without hesitation quickly return to the *Fabulous Four Link* questions. Stay focused. If you do not, soon the person you are talking to is in control of the conversation and your reason for attending is forgotten.

Preparation Precedes Prosperity

Miracle 65

The Clusters

The **Cluster Questions** (refer to the definition page) are a combination of seven **Little Miracles** which are used to determine if the stranger is a Link possibility. The Cluster Questions include a bridge question, four Link questions, and two conclusions. Conversation Conclusion One (**Little Miracle 72**) is used when you want to meet the stranger again. Conversation Conclusion Two (**Little Miracle 73**) is used when you do not wish to begin a relationship. The stranger may be a great person but not a great Link. Conclude Conversation Conclusion Two with care. Leave every stranger with the sincere feeling you were pleased to meet them. You may meet them on the way down. The Cluster Question process brings prosperity that is perpetual because Links are continually giving you business until the relationship ends. To read these **Little Miracles** is meaningless. To apply them is everything.

Prosperity is a process

Miracle

The Bridge

The bridge is an important segment of the *Prosperity Process*. The bridge is a connection between the handshake and the Link questions. The bridge must be well constructed. The bridge must contain one innocuous question that melts the ice, but do not lose focus on your mission of discovering Links. The bridge question must be disarming. This makes a smooth transition from the handshake to the Link questions. I have four bridge suggestions: **1)** "How did you hear about the event?" **2)** "Did you have difficulty finding a parking spot?" **3)** "Have you attended these meetings before?" **4)** "What do you know about the speaker?" After one innocuous question, begin asking the four Link questions.

The bridge connects strangers

Miracle 67

Four and No More

The next four **Little Miracles** will be devoted to Link questions. They will open new windows of opportunities. The *Fabulous Four Link* questions will change the financial direction of your career forever! You must ask these critical questions of everyone. These questions will determine the Link possibility of everyone. These questions are Link questions, not prospect questions. Links are multiple. Prospects are singular. Be precise. Be concise. Be resolute. Be focused. This process requires a 180° shift in your communication paradigm. It may seem awkward at first, but also once mastered, you will find the questions not only become comfortable but also very, very profitable. You have arrived when meeting other professionals without the Link questions is the same as going golfing without your putter.

Prosperity is a process

Miracle 68

Link Question One

Link Question One will catapult you from *Penury to Prosperity*. The first question is, **"What does your firm do?"** This question is designed to assist you in your search for the elusive Link. Each of the four Link questions will not only help you determine if that professional is a Link, but will also eliminate those who are not. Many times the answer to this question will give you a Link clue. For example, if the answer to this question is, "My firm builds air conditioners for office buildings" you know that they interface with a multitude of disciplines including, architects, construction companies, developers, tenants of office buildings, and janitorial services. If your target market interfaces with these industries, you have a similar client base. I suggest a *Link Lunch*.

Stop taking the vow of poverty

Miracle

Link Question Two

Link Question Two is, **"What is your position with your firm?"** This question continues the process of discovering the ultimate business contact, a Link. If the professional says, "I'm the CEO of Smith & Sons," you know you are communicating with the supreme decision maker. A *Link Lunch* is an imperative. If the answer to **Link Question Two** is, "I just started with my firm last week," that person may have little clout. A luncheon chat could be a waste of time and money. However, if the person recently moved from a firm, the professional may have been a decision maker with their previous firm. You may need further querying. That person may have Link potential.

Condense time, expand money

Miracle

Link Question Three

I f **Link Question One** or **Link Question Two** do not ferret out a Link possibility, this **Little Miracle** will. This question is a million dollars in a bottle, just waiting for you to pull the cork. Link Question Three is, **"What is your target market?"** If your target market is similar to their target market and you are not in competition, you may have a Link. A great example is XEROX and AT&T. Both firms call on similar businesses but sell a different product. Firms which need a copier often need a new phone system. This is a perfect match. This could be a fabulous Link. When you develop twelve Links in twelve diverse industries, you are in financial Nirvana.

Stop being a Prisoner of Poverty

Miracle 71

Link Question Four

This question is not the highest priority but is very effective in determining which professionals to target as Link possibilities. **Link Question Four** is, **"How long have you been with your firm?"** If they have been with their firm for thirty days, they may not have developed business contacts in their industry. However, a professional moving from one firm to another may possess Link possibilities. If they have been with their firm for twelve years, they most likely have a *Multitude of Merchants* in their Rolodex. Determine which professional is worth the price of a lunch. You buy. Do not commit the Link questions to memory, commit them to life!

Condense time, expand money

72 Miracle

Conversation Conclusion One

This concludes The Clusters One. This is the conclusion you use when you want to see the person again. When you find a potential Link, don't say, "I want to come over to your office and tell you about a new product line we are introducing." That is *Financial Foolishness*. You are selling. Begin by giving. Make a 180° paradigm shift in your communication exchange and say, **"May I have your card? I will give you a call tomorrow. Let's get together and see if we can help each other develop some business. It was a pleasure to meet you,"** and move on. A Wells Fargo Senior Vice President shared this gem in one of his lectures: "We are not in the transaction business. We are in the relationship business."

Receiving is the fruit of a seed

Miracle

Conversation Conclusion Two

This concludes The Clusters Two. This is the conclusion you use when a person does not represent a business opportunity. Some conversations need a conclusion sooner than others. If the conversation is going nowhere and keeps going around and around like a merry-go-round and ends where you began, terminate it quickly! I give you four suggestions to terminate a conversation: **1)** "I've enjoyed meeting you. I know you have other people you would like to meet and I've others I would like to meet. I'm looking forward to seeing you again." **2)** "Where are the hors d'oeuvres?" **3)** Introduce the person you are terminating to another and make a graceful exit. **4)** "Where is the restroom?" I have discovered termination number one to be the most effective. End the communication exchange within five minutes and begin another. This **Little Miracle** is better than winning the lottery.

A conclusion can be a beginning

Miracle 74

Second-Tier Questions

Add these four questions to make sure you are choosing the best professional for a Link: **1)** "How long has your firm been in business?" **2)** "How many employees does your firm have?" **3)** "How many offices?" **4)** "What is your territory?" Before you leave your office for an event, write down all these questions. I have a trilogy to follow. Endorse the questions. Embody the questions. Execute the questions. Because networking takes time, you must plant in the spring if you want a harvest in the fall. If you don't plant in the spring, you will beg in the fall.

Begging is for paupers

Miracle

Avoidance Questions

Avoid questions where you lose control. If you control the questions, you control the answers. Avoid the George Burns question. He would begin each performance with, "Gracie, how's your brother?" The Gracie monologue would continue for twenty two minutes. I have four avoidance questions: **1)** "How's your golf game?" **2)** "Where are you going on your vacation?" **3)** "How is the family?" **4)** "What do you think of the Dodgers?" These questions will take up all of the thirty minutes of the Social Hour. The gavel will come down on the sounding board and you will be asked to take your seat. The gavel has also come down on your career. You have created a problem: Do I keep their card or toss it?

Purify the process

Miracle 76

Meetings to Money

There are six requirements that will convert *Meetings to Money*:

1) **Read** the **Little Miracles**
2) **Learn** the **Little Miracles**
3) **Apply** the **Little Miracles**
4) **Own** the **Little Miracles**
5) **Share** the **Little Miracles**
6) **Teach** the **Little Miracles**

These **Little Miracles** can only enter a mind that is not filled to capacity with archaic marketing concepts. Without using these six requirements, you will never transport the **Little Miracles** from your *Mind to your Molecules*. Make **Little Miracles** a part of your *Marketing Metric*. When you do, you will convert *Contacts to Cash*.

You learn what you teach

Miracle

Strictly Social

When I was the Marketing Director of the Wilshire Chamber of Commerce in Los Angeles, I attended all the social events. I asked a realtor at a chamber mixer, "May I have your business card?" He gave me a puzzled look and responded, "I didn't bring any cards. I thought the mixer was Strictly Social." Stop justifying your failures. According to the latest research, at least 13% of all the people attending every social event are fertile soil for your *Business Bounty*. Why walk in the opposite direction of your dreams? You can't turn east to see the sunset. Don't allow the sun to set on your financial goals and dreams. Don't let the sun set on your stacks and stacks of *Luscious Lucre*. You are beginning the journey of transforming idle chatter and chance encounters into multiple business opportunities.

Success is intentional

78 Miracle

Everyone is a Peer

It is important to remember when you are networking that everyone has to be perceived as a peer. Unless you check your ego at the door, your future goes out the window. Rip off your corporate badge of ego and treat everyone as an equal. A business baron or a busboy, a CEO or a secretary, a judge or a janitor are all equal. It makes no difference. Information is the key. Information levels the playing field. A secretary with her finger on the hold button knows more than any CEO will ever disclose. You cannot see eye to eye when you are looking down your nose at another.

You choose, ego or economics

Miracle

79

The Five-Minute Waltz

I equate discovering Links with dancing around an event. Spend no more than five minutes with each stranger you meet. Then waltz on to the next professional. Be careful, do not become as a tornado through a Kansas cornfield. Be as smooth as a politician at a fund-raiser. With practice you become subtle, smooth, succinct, and successful. At the end of three hundred seconds, no matter what, move on. Use **The Cluster Questions** (refer to the definition page) and you will know if that professional is a possible Link, a prospect, a new friend, a resource person, or without financial value. After five minutes, waltz on.

Follow the music when you waltz

Miracle 80

Financial Fraud

If you take more than five minutes with anyone at a Social Hour, you are committing *Financial Fraud*. You are stealing from yourself. This is typical flat-earth thinking. There are many reasons professionals spend too many minutes with each person. None has validity. They are not reasons, they are excuses. Business men and women spend twenty minutes with one professional because of any one of the three following excuses: **1)** Many people allow others to monopolize the conversation. **2)** Some want to begin a rapport. **3)** Most have no agenda. Unless you move from stranger to stranger every five minutes during the Social Hour, you will miss at least one stranger who has a bulging Rolodex (Contact List) full of your prospects waiting just for you. Why keep wasting your financial life?

If time be money, conserve it

Miracle
81
Your Alimentary Canal

I believe God gave us guts. Not just for assimilating food, but to assist us in allaying our fears. Madame Curie wrote, "There is nothing to be feared, only understood." William Shakespeare scribed, "Act the part and you become it." Ralph Waldo Emerson so eloquently stated, "Assume a virtue though you have it not." Helen Keller wrote, "Life is a bold adventure or it is nothing at all." Joe Paterno, a brilliant football coach, told his new tailback, "When you cross the goal line act as if you have been there one hundred times before." If life never offered challenges, how would you ever discover guts? When you have entered one hundred events, shaken one thousand hands, and used **The Cluster Questions** (refer to definition page) at least a thousand times, your alimentary canal will have purged your fears.

Fear is a habit

Miracle 82

Bonanza or Bust?

Are you wasting valuable time at each event? At each event you have one hundred and twenty minutes to harvest your financial hay. You have a thirty-minute social time, a thirty-minute lunch time, and a sixty-minute speaker time. The one hundred and twenty minutes you have at each event can be a *Bonanza or a Bust*. If you add a thirty-minute drive to the event, a thirty-minute drive back to your office, and you are careless with your **Little Miracles**, you have wasted three hours. It is your choice to win or to lose. The coin is on your thumb. Flip it with prudence.

You don't waste time, you lose it

Miracle

Your Financial Cup

As a child you enter this Universe with an empty cup. As a child your mind is unencumbered. It fills up quickly. As you become an adult, your cup of knowledge is so full of obsolete data that little new and productive information can enter your financial cup. Empty your marketing cup! You have to remove old, hardened, and antiquated marketing concepts to increase your market share. Peter Drucker preached, "Ancient marketing concepts linger on long after their productive life." Empty your brain of all your archaic marketing habits. When you replace your 19th century marketing habits with **Little Miracles** your cup will runneth over with currency.

A full cup receiveth nothing

Miracle 84

A Room Full of Whos?

One hundred percent of all professionals who have not studied the **Little Miracles** do not know the answer to this question. I answer this question with a question: "If you had a magic wand and had only one wish, which professionals would you want at the next meeting you attend?" One hundred percent would answer with alacrity, "Those who would buy my product or service." That is prospecting. Continue to peel the bulb. Make a 180° shift in your *Marketing Mind*. Would you rather have a room full of professionals who would buy from you or a room full of professionals who have a Rolodex full of people who would buy from you? You have no options. The answer is transparently clear.

Food for a day or feast for a life

Miracle 85

Defer Your Rapport

When does rapport begin? Rapport certainly does not begin at an event. I am not against building rapport. I recommend you defer it. Think on this: if there are one hundred attending an event, during the thirty-minute Social Hour you cannot begin one hundred rapports. It is impossible to develop rapport with even one person. Rapport takes time. You do not have the luxury of time at an event. You only have thirty minutes of social time. It is not rapport time. It is screening time. You develop rapport with people the same way you eat grapes, one at a time. Use **The Cluster Questions** (refer to the definition page) and you will select at least one professional with whom to have a *Link Lunch*.

Rapport begins at lunch

Miracle

The Link Legend

You become a Link Legend when you make developing Links your number one priority. If this is your commitment, it is necessary for you to perceive the economic importance of the **Little Miracles**. Listen to Michael Korda, Editor-in-Chief of Simon and Schuster: Establish a network. If you are over forty and haven't friends who rely on you and to whom you can turn, you are in trouble. These are colleagues for whom you do favors, whose projects you support, whose problems you listen to, and they do the same for you. A network is not something you can establish overnight. It takes decades of nurturing. In business you need lots of people, spread out in the right places, whom you can depend on because they can depend on you."

Becoming a legend is a process

Miracle

The Watering Hole

Everyone has a professional they need to meet. Some executives will not return your phone calls. Everyone you need to meet has a favorite watering hole. Search for the events they frequent. I have four suggestions:

1) Charities they patronize
2) Associations where they are members
3) After-hours social affairs
4) Their favorite attitude adjustment pub

All these suggestions are reservoirs of business. This **Little Miracle** collapses the time between the *Search and the Sale.*

Quench your financial thirst

Miracle

Begin Each Appointment with a Gift

Nothing is more productive than beginning each appointment with a gift. I have always been taught in sales courses to ask for five referrals on every sales call. No relationship begins by getting. You may get five referrals, but that is all. If you begin by giving five referrals you will get ten referrals. Go beyond referrals. Give an idea that will improve the person's cash flow. Give a book that will increase their revenue. The **Little Miracles** will do just fine. I suggest you have the gift professionally wrapped. The person receiving the gift will be impressed. The wrap elevates you to a zone above your competitors. There are three financial advantages when you begin each appointment with a gift: 1) A professional will open their Rolodex sooner. 2) A professional will open their pocketbook quicker. 3) A client will remain a client longer. This **Little Miracle** will make you wealthy beyond your wildest imaginings.

Receiving is the offspring of giving

Miracle 89

Marketing Time vs. Client Time

Think of marketing time AS more important than client time. Clients have a way of disappearing. Clients leave you for many reasons. They leave because firms merge. They leave because clients transfer. They leave because clients are terminated. They leave because clients retire. They leave because clients expire. US News and World report has a chart on why clients leave.

- 1% die
- 3% move away
- 5% other friends
- 9% competition
- 14% poor service
- 68% staff indifference

Look at your client list of five years ago. Look at your client list today. Was there any attrition? It is not what you are going through but what you are going to. Go to the **Little Miracles**.

The solution is in the problem

Miracle 90

Outlaw the Walkman

The Walkman or iPod MP3 player should be outlawed. Walking is a time to listen to the instructions from God. When you are listening to noise, God cannot get through. When you are listening to noise, God gets a busy signal. When you are listening to noise, God's gifts for you are given to another. Noise interferes with your good. Noise is defined by Fillmore as "The dying vibration of a spent force." Noise is garbage. You don't have to be in the sanitation business to know garbage. Think on this: if Moses had been wearing a Walkman, would he have parted the sea? Would Jesus have recorded the Beatitudes? Would the Wright Brothers have conquered flight? Would Newton have discovered gravity? What great good are you denying yourself and others when you wear a Walkman?

You choose, God or garbage?

Miracle

Spring Training

Before the Los Angeles Dodgers begin their regular season, they used to head to Vero Beach, Florida, for six weeks of spring training. *Business and Baseball* are similar. You have to spend a few weeks in spring training. You must practice with people who have no impact on your career. To develop new habits you must practice six weeks before you greet an important executive. Practice **The Cluster Questions** (refer to definition page) with your wife, husband, children, uncles, aunts, grandpa, grandma, waitress, waiter, shoeshine person, bellman, busboy, and the grocery bag person. Practice with anything that moves or breathes. Your skills must move from first nature to second nature.

Second nature is discipline

Miracle 92

The Rhino Response

Stop charging past business opportunities. You are not a rhinoceros. Stop charging past strangers to greet a friend. Be aware of all the strangers around you. If they have a name tag, look at the firm name. Do you need a contact in that industry? If you do, extend your hand and ask **The Cluster Questions** (refer to definition page). Within sixty seconds you will know if a stranger has Link potential. Even though this professional may be a good Link, move on within five minute because one of the next five professionals you meet may have one hundred or more of your future clients in their Rolodex. Now, think beyond meetings. Stop using the *Rhino Response* (charging past business opportunities) in elevators, hallways, parking lots, ATM machines, and stores of all sizes. Many of these people in these places have great economic potential. Miss them at your own fiscal peril.

Stop living in a zoo

Miracle

Talk to Anyone

Talk to anyone who is not a felon. In other words, talk to everyone, everywhere, all the time. I have developed Links from professionals I met in corridors, elevators, restrooms, restaurants, markets, sports bars, churches, synagogues, Kiwanis, Chambers of Commerce, American Heart, American Lung, American Diabetes, Red Cross, United Way, and on and on and on. Make the following commitment now: "I will talk to everyone, everywhere, all the time until the Dead Sea becomes alive."

Stop treating everyone as a felon

Miracle

The Restroom Affair

Speak to people in restrooms. Most people disagree. Many people assume this is a solitary experience. Most assumptions are wrong. Here is an illustration to prove my concept. A quote from a Beverly Hills intellectual property attorney: "I greeted a person in the restroom whom I had often seen on the same floor of my office building. I had never spoken to him before. Because of your seminar, I spoke to him. We talked. I found he was an ophthalmologist and an inventor. We exchanged business cards. The next day he called me. He is now a client of mine." A restroom can be a positive experience.

Comfort stations are profit stations

Miracle

Your Million-Dollar Rolodex

Begin at the end. The end result of any transaction is in your Rolodex. Thumb through your million-dollar Rolodex. What is the profession of each of your clients? Record each profession. Go back three to five years. Prioritize your clients' professions by percentages. Here is an example:

1. Commercial Realtors...................46%
2. New businesses..........................18%
3. Insurance Brokers......................16%
4. Small Businesses........................12%
5. Senior Citizens..........................8%

Now you have your target market, commercial realtors. Begin to visit organizations and associations whose members are commercial realtors or better yet, visit meetings which are populated with professionals who have a Rolodex full of commercial realtors.

Spin your Rolodex for revenue

Miracle

The Miracle Mile

An ancient mystic, over two hundred centuries ago, taught his followers to go the second mile. In the days of the Roman Empire soldiers could require the peasants to carry their packs one mile. The Christians would carry a soldier's pack two miles. Because of the Christians' passion for their faith, many Roman soldiers were converted to Christianity. Carry the burdens of your clients, your customers, your prospects, your business friends, and your Links an extra mile. You will have more business than your *Till can Tolerate*. Going the second mile is a *Pragmatic Principle*. Harvey Mackay goes the second mile. Harvey inked the following, "We have to spend as much time promoting our customers' products as we do our own."

Your second mile has no Sig-Alerts

Miracle 97

The Backup Process

Before you leave your office for an event, have a backup. Have a second professional as an alternate whom you would like to meet. If priority number one does not show or has someone sitting on both sides or has brought a guest, move to your backup. This is priority number two. This allows you to sit by someone of financial importance in your *Quest for Cash*. For financial safety, add priority number three. Do not leave your financial destiny to chance. Your life is not a movie. You cannot rewind an event and begin from the beginning. Never leave any event with an empty purse.

Have a backup for your backup

Miracle 98

Unbearable Mediocrity

Mediocrity is self-inflicted. Mediocrity is self-imposed. Mediocrity is a habit. Don't become an indentured servant to a habit. Mediocrity is the result of *Flabby Focus*. Are you getting frustrated watching the financial parade pass you by? I disagree with Will Rogers. Will advised us, "Someone has to sit on the curb and applaud as the parade goes by." Don't let that someone be you! Would you rather be a spectator or a participant? Would you rather have lunchmeat or lobster? Would you rather have a VW or a BMW? Would you rather have a Suzuki or a Seville? When the pain of mediocrity becomes unbearable, you will take some productive action. You will become *Money Motivated*.

Mediocre people worry me

Miracle

Sever the Umbilical Cord

Most professionals walk around each event with a friend. An invisible umbilical cord keeps them from separating. They walk together. They talk together. They laugh together. They sit together. They go to the restroom together. They leave together. And they go through Chapter 11 together. If you are always with a friend, you meet no one. You gather neither business nor information when shackled to a friend. Unless you loosen the restraint, the curtain will come down on your mediocre career. Stop following your peers. Most peers defer to peers. Most peers are uninformed. Most peers are mediocre. When you sever the umbilical cord to your friend you will experience both fear and thrill. The fear of being alone at an event, the thrill of meeting new people, and the thrill of meeting new money.

Cut the Cord of Conformity

Miracle 100

God has No Grandchildren

WOW! This means no one is closer to God than you. God wants to give you the keys to the Kingdom. The Universe is ready to give you all you ever asked for. All you ever desired. Don't pray for more things. Pray for a larger capacity. Ask your Maker for a larger container to hold all the lavish, inexhaustible goodies God has for you. We are all equally close to the abundant, copious, and unlimited wealth of the Universe. I see nothing but good in the Kingdom. Your keys to the Kingdom are not lost, just mislaid.

God never changes the locks

The Evolved Link

As you become immersed in the **Little Miracles**, the first question that enters your mind when questioning a stranger is, **"Which one of my Links could benefit from knowing this   person?"**

When you lose yourself in the **Little Miracles**, you begin to care more about your Links' success than your own and for some mysterious reason, in the process, you become wealthy.

It takes much self-discipline, much focus, and much commitment.

"You are the CEO of your financial destiny."

Mel Kaufmann

A Prosperity PAK

A **PAK** is a gathering of a few committed business professionals to assist each other in reaching their goals and dreams. Gather around a cup of coffee and study the **Little Miracles**. The Little Miracles is a quick read but lifetime study. Study a few **Little Miracles** weekly with your business associates. Begin each **PAK** by having everyone share the successes and challenges they encountered by practicing the **Little Miracles**.

The following are a few questions to ask at each **PAK** meeting, after reading each Little Miracle:

What insights did you learn from this Little Miracle?
Where can you use this Little Miracle?
When can you begin using the Little Miracle?
How will this Little Miracle increase your cash flow?
Does this Little Miracle have any personal relevance?

The only requirement of each **PAK** member is to purcahse the book of **Little Miracles**. When any **PAK** member believes they are ready to become a teacher, they can begin a new **PAK**.

The Complete Set of EspressoBrian.com Business Success Tools

Visit our website today and learn about all of the EspressoBrain.com tools and The **Little Miracles**.

The EspressoBrain Products

Little Miracles   EspressoBrain Café
Prosperity PAK   Professional Networking PAK

Connect With Us

Facebook.com/EspressoBrain
Twitter.com/EspressoBrain

Join our live FREE weekly Conference Call

We have a live discussion about The Little Miracles with others around the country! Go to EspressoBrain. com to sign up to be notified.

Sign up for our newsletter today!

EspressoBrain.com

If you follow our networking steps, then Financial Freedom among other things is truly accessible to you.

Thank you,
Team EspressoBrain.com

A Place For Your Notes

A Place For Your Notes

A Place For Your Notes

A Place For Your Notes

Made in the USA
Lexington, KY
26 September 2013